W9-ARX-189

HANDY HOUSEHOLD HINTS

Tips & Techniques

A money saving manual for household maintenance and repairs

Published by
AMI Group Books
Boulder Colorado

Published by AMI Group Books, Inc.
P.O. Box 7306, Boulder, Colorado 80306.

ISBN 0-9767494-0-8

Printed in the USA

GOT A GOOD TIP?
We want you to be part of our book. If you have discovered or had passed on to you a tip you think our readers can use please send it to the publisher. If we use your tip in the book we will give you credit as a 'Contributor'. If we receive the same tip from more than one person we will credit the one with the earliest post mark. Tips should be 100 words or less and must be able to be accomplished by the average home owner without using dangerous chemicals or specialized tools. Please e-mail your tips to: info@HandymanDenver.com or mail them to the publisher at: AMI Group Books, P.O. Box 7306, Boulder, Colorado 80306

CAUTION
All home projects involve a degree of risk. Skills, materials, tools, and site conditions vary widely. Our editors have made every effort to ensure accuracy; however, the reader remains responsible for the selection and use of tools, materials, and methods. Please follow manufacturers' operating instructions and observe safety precautions. Solvents, chemicals and compounds react differently to different materials; the user should do a test on a small area to determine if satisfactory results will be achieved.

CONTENTS

Shop at the store nearest you
(Stores are listed alphabetically by city)
ACE®
THE HELPFUL PLACE®

Ralston Ace Hardware
9447 W. 57th Ave.
Arvada, CO 80002
303-424-4202

Sheridan Ace Hardware
5017 W. 64th Ave.
Arvada, CO 80003
303-426-1035

Ace Hardware of Arvada
8031 Wadsworth Blvd.
Arvada, CO 80003
303-463-4992

Hoffman Heights Ace
Hardware
644 Peoria St.
Aurora, CO 80011
303-366-3524

Moore Lumber & Ace
Hardware
5195 County Road 64
Bailey, CO 80421
303-838-5362

Greatwood Lumber &
Hardware
1555 S. 1st St.
Bennett, CO 80102
303-644-5000

Ace Hardware of Boulder
2486 Baseline Rd.
Boulder, CO 80305
303-443-1616

American Pride Ace Hardware
55 W. Bromley Lane
Brighton, CO 80601
303-659-1230

Big Tool Box
8080 S. Holly St.
Centennial, CO 80122
303-779-8822

Commerce City Ace Hardware
East 69th & Highway 85
Commerce City, CO 80022
303-288-6641

Aspen Park Hardware Inc
26572 Barkley Rd.
Conifer, CO 80433
303-697-4778

University Hills Ace Hardware
2500 S. Colorado Blvd.
Denver, CO 80222
303-759-0980

Perl-Mack Ace Hardware
7041 Pecos St.
Denver, CO 80221
303-429-2944

Ninth Ave. Ace Hardware
1030 E. 9th Ave.
Denver, CO 80218
303-831-7066

12th Ave. Ace Hardware
2640 E. 12th Ave.
Denver, CO 80206
303-355-2551

Fairfax Ace Hardware
5100-10 E. Colfax Ave.
Denver, CO 80220
303-320-6551

Tamarac Square Ace
Hardware
7777 E. Hampden Ave.
Denver, CO 80231
303-751-7225

Edgewater Ace Hardware
1977 Sheridan Blvd.
Edgewater, CO 80214
303-233-4810

A&A Tradin Post Elizabeth
175 W. Kiowa Ave.
Elizabeth, CO 80107
303-646-9366

A&A Tradin Post Englewood
4509 S. Broadway
Englewood, CO 80110
303-761-0747

Ace Hardware of Firestone
8258 County Rd 13
Firestone, CO 80504
303-833-9191

Highlands Ranch Ace
Hardware
9579 S. University Blvd.
Highlands Ranch, CO 80126
303-683-6300

Lafayette Ace Hardware
900 S. Highway 287
Lafayette, CO 80026
720-890-9888

Green Mountain Ace Hardware
12035 W. Alameda Parkway
Lakewood, CO 80228
303-988-1883

Lake Ridge Ace Hardware
2563 Kipling St.
Lakewood, CO 80215
303-231-9400

Kipling Ace Hardware
5914 S. Kipling St.
Littleton, CO 80127
303-978-9048

Littleton Ace Hardware
6905 S. Broadway
Littleton, CO 80122
303-795-9469

A&A Tradin Post Columbine
6720 S. Pierce St.
Littleton, CO 80128
303-948-8813

Ace Hardware of Longmont
1727 N. Main St.
Longmont, CO 80501
303-776-5173

Indian Peaks Ace Hardware
74 Highway 119 South
Nederland, CO 80466
303-258-3132

Mission Trace Ace Hardware
3851 E. 120th Ave.
Thornton, CO 80241
303-252-1776

For additional Colorado locations, go to:
www.AceHardware.com

INTRODUCTION

This book is for anyone who has ever strolled the grocery aisle and wondered, "Who buys that 10-pound box of baking soda?" or paid a plumber $90 to come out and flip the reset button on the garbage disposal. You learn a lot when you take care of a house. The problem is that many of the lessons cost too much or are learned too late.

You'll find the kinds of tips I wish I'd known about when I bought my first house. Nothing complicated – just quick, easy things you can do to maintain a home, grouped by areas of the house and alphabetized for easy reference. Best of all, most of the instructions call for using inexpensive items you might already have around the house.

My partner, John Champagne, and I have been repairing and remodeling homes for over 30 years, and have more than 70 craftsmen working in the Denver area. We started compiling these tips in response to questions from our customers. Some of the tips are handyman essentials; others are as old (and as good) as the advice my grandmother gave me when I moved into my first apartment. I hope you'll find them as useful as I have.

My best,
Orley Paxton

ACKNOWLEDGEMENTS

The partners at COSJ Inc., John & Claudean Champagne and Orley & Sheila Paxton, would like to thank Ron Davis and the many craftspeople who submitted tips for this book, including Tom Treadwell, Ed McLaughlin, David Bright, Ron Heselton, Wayne Svenson, Patrick M. Dever and Larry Drees. Special thanks to Julie Paxton, Dawn Young, and Jill Bielawski for sorting through all the tips and editing the book. Thanks also to Mark Middleton (mark@paperherodesign.com), for the wonderful illustrations.

BATHROOMS

BATHTUBS, ENAMEL

To whiten an enamel bathtub, rub it with a solution of salt and turpentine.

To remove stains, make a paste of 3 tablespoons cream of tartar mixed with 1 tablespoon hydrogen peroxide. Wipe the paste on the stains with a soft cloth and scrub them away.

To remove brown iron stains, rub the stains with a cut lemon that has been dipped in salt.

BATHTUB, FIBERGLASS

Clean a fiberglass tub with white vinegar. Simply heat the vinegar, pour it into a spray bottle, spray it on the tub, and wipe it off with a soft cloth. Wait 10 or 15 minutes, and then pour more white vinegar on a clean sponge and scrub the entire tub. Rinse well and dry.

BRUSHES, CLEANING

Clean and sterilize hairbrushes, combs, and clips by soaking them in a solution of 3 cups ammonia mixed with 1 cup water. After they have soaked in the solution for 30 minutes, rinse them in cold water.

DRAIN, FRESHEN

To freshen a drain, pour one-fourth cup baking soda down the drain, followed by one-half cup white vinegar. Cover the drain tightly for a few minutes, and then flush with cold water.

DRAIN, CLOGGED

See "Plumbing" section.

DRAIN, PROTECTION

Place a piece of steel wool over unprotected drains to stop hair from clogging the drain.

FIXTURES

Use a fabric softener sheet for day-to-day cleaning.

If you need more cleaning power, spray a rag with white vinegar. Rub the fixtures, wipe dry, and buff with a soft cloth.

To remove lime or hard-water buildup, rub fixtures with lemon juice or vinegar, and then rinse. Be careful not to leave the solution on too long, or it may cause damage.

FIXTURES, COPPER AND BRASS

Sprinkle salt on half a lemon and rub it on copper and brass fixtures to get them clean. *See illustration opposite*

FIXTURES, CHROME

To polish chrome, use dry baking soda on a soft cloth.

To remove rust spots, rub them with aluminum foil and then wipe with a dry cloth. For extra cleaning power, first dip the aluminum in Coke® or Pepsi®.

GROUT, CLEANING

If your grout is colored, use straight vinegar. If your grout is white, use bleach or hydrogen peroxide. Scrub with an old toothbrush.

GROUT, REPLACING

If your tile needs a face-lift, consider replacing the grout. It's a relatively easy, do-it-yourself project that will renew the look of your bathroom.

MOLD AND MILDEW

Keep humidity low and allow air to circulate to
prevent mildew.

To prevent mold growth, spray shower walls with
white vinegar every couple of days.

To get rid of mildew, mix 1 part baking soda with 1
part bleach (use rubber gloves).

To remove mildew from the corners of a shower or
bathtub, dip cotton balls in bleach and let them sit on
the mildew for a few minutes. Then remove the cotton
balls and rinse the corners well.

ORGANIZATION TIPS

Attach magnets to the inside doors of your medicine
cabinet to hold metal items such as tweezers and
fingernail clippers.

Heat and steam can ruin medicine. Move all of your
medicine from the medicine cabinet to the kitchen.

Use decorative baskets with lids to keep bulky items
such as hair dryers and curling irons out of sight.

If you have young children, use a mesh laundry bag to
keep tub toys from taking over a bathroom. After the bath,
hang the mesh bag over the tub to allow toys to drip dry.

SHAVING CREAM CANS, RUST PREVENTION

Put a can of shaving cream into a beer/soda coozie (a beverage insulator) to prevent the can from leaving rust rings on sinks, tubs, and shower floors.

SHOWER DOORS, CLEANING

After cleaning, spray shower doors with a product made for automobile windshields to sheet rain. Your shower doors will stay clean much longer because it will be harder for grime to stick.

To clean soap scum from shower doors, pour lemon oil on a soft cloth. Rub the oil on both sides of the doors. Then use a scrubbing sponge to remove the buildup.

To clean the shower track door, pour full-strength vinegar into the track, let it soak for a few minutes, and then rinse.

SHOWERHEAD, CLOGGED

If your showerhead is clogged with hard-water deposits, soak it in undiluted white vinegar overnight. To avoid removing the showerhead, pour the vinegar in a plastic sandwich bag and tie the bag around the showerhead. Remove the bag the next morning and use an old toothbrush to scrub away the mineral deposits. *See illustration previous page*

STEAM, REMOVAL

After stepping out of a hot shower, turn the cold water on full blast for a few moments to help clear steam from the bathroom.

TOILET, NOT FLUSHING

See "Plumbing" section.

TOILET BOWL, CLEANING

Pour one-fourth cup bleach in the toilet bowl to clean it while you're away for the day. (Do not use this method if you're already using a tank-held cleaner; the chemicals released with that cleaner might react with the bleach.)

To avoid clogging and odors, pour 1 cup baking soda down the bowl each week.

TUB, CAULKING

To replace caulk, first remove the old sealant using a flathead screwdriver – just be careful not to scratch the tub or tile. Then clean and dry the area so the new sealant will adhere. *See illustration*

To apply the new caulk, fill the tub with water. (The weight ensures that the tub will be at its lowest point when you apply the sealant). Next create a guide for applying the caulk by putting painter's tape or masking tape around the edges of both the tub and the tile. Fill the gap with silicone caulking. Wear rubber gloves and use your finger to smooth any uneven caulking. Remove the tape. Next use a damp rag to wipe away any excess caulking. Let the new caulk dry overnight (or up to 24 hours), and then drain the water from the tub.

WALLS, CLEANING

To clean bathroom walls, first close the doors and windows and run hot water in the tub or shower to create steam. This makes it easier to clean the walls.

WATER STAINS, HARD

Apply white vinegar to hard-water stains on tile and shower doors. Rinse after 10 minutes.

CAR AND GARAGE

APPLICATORS, DISPOSABLE
Keep a box of tongue depressors (available at pharmacies) to use as disposable applicators for glue or paint.

AUTOMATIC DOOR, SENSOR TESTING
Use a roll of paper towels to test the sensor on an automatic garage door. Open the door all the way and then put a roll of paper towels on its side directly in the path of the door. Close the garage door. When the door reaches the roll of paper towels, it should reverse and open back up. If the door crushes the paper towels, the safety reverse mechanism needs to be adjusted. Consult your owner's manual or call a professional. *See illustration next page*

CAR, BATTERY
Clean a car battery's terminals with baking soda and water to prevent the battery from becoming covered with acid. Let the terminals dry and then rub petroleum jelly on them to prevent corrosion.

CAR, CLEANING
Mix 2 tablespoons baking soda with a quart of warm water to clean the exterior of a car. Hose the car down afterward to rinse it well.

To remove dried gasoline stains, mix a tablespoon of kerosene with a cup of water. Rub the solution on the stains with a soft cloth, rinse, and buff dry.

CAR, EMERGENCY LIGHTS

In case of emergency, keep a couple of red balloons and a flashlight in the glove compartment. If you need warning lights, slip a balloon over the flashlight.

CAR KEYS, BROKEN

If a car key breaks off in the lock, coat the broken end with the type of glue used for mounting sanding disks (available in hardware or home improvement stores) and insert what's left of the key gently into the lock. Once it connects with the broken piece inside the lock, pull the key out. The broken tip should stick to the glue and come out.

CAR, PAINT TOUCH-UP

Use shoe polish to touch up worn spots on a car's finish. Rub the polish in with a soft cloth and then cover the spot with auto wax.

CAR, REARVIEW MIRROR

Use foam shaving cream to clean the rearview mirror. It not only cleans it, but it also adds an anti-fog coating on the surface.

CHROME, CLEANING

To remove grime and rust spots, rub chrome with aluminum foil and then wipe with a dry cloth. For extra cleaning power, first dip the foil in Coke® or Pepsi®.

CONCRETE FLOORS, CLEANING

Use a strong solution of degreaser to clean dirty concrete floors in the garage. Flood the floor and let the solution stand for a few minutes before scrubbing it with a nylon brush. Use a squeegee to push the solution and grime to one area of the garage. Pick it up with an old dustpan and then use a hose to rinse the floor. You might have to repeat the process to clean an extremely dirty floor.

CONCRETE FLOORS, OIL STAINS

Sprinkle new oil spots on concrete with kitty litter. After the litter absorbs the oil, sweep the area clean. Next scrub the stain with liquid dish soap and water. You may have to scrub the area several times before the oil is completely gone. (Use a nylon bristle scrubbing brush. A wire brush might scratch the concrete finish and leave a permanent scar.)

To try to remove old oil stains, make a thick paste with automatic dishwashing soap and water. Leave it on the stain overnight and then scrub with a nylon brush and rinse.

GARAGE DOOR, MAINTENANCE

Wipe the garage door down with a soft cloth and a mild cleanser every six months. This will help prevent damage such as rusting caused by dirt and other debris sticking to the door.

After you clean, check for any broken or bent components and lubricate all moving parts. Then tighten all screws and nuts.

Apply car wax to the door to repel dirt and moisture.

GARDEN TOOLS, STORAGE

To prevent rust and corrosion, store small garden tools in a bucket of clean, dry sand for the winter.

HANDS, OIL REMOVAL

To clean oil stains from your hands and under your fingernails, scrub them with a damp nailbrush dipped in baking soda.

HOOKS

Hang a three-pronged soil cultivator upside down on the wall to make three wall hooks. Hang a few in a row if you need more hooks.

STORAGE, BULKY ITEMS

String a strong net from the ceiling at the back of the garage (where it will not interfere with the garage door). Use it to store bulky, lightweight items such as sleeping bags, badminton nets, and artificial wreaths.

STORAGE, SMALL PARTS

Attach jar lids to the underside of a shelf with a couple of screws and fill the jars with nails, screws, and other small parts. Twist the jars on and you'll have a row of easy-to-access storage that's out of the way of your work area. *See illustration next page*

TAR, REMOVAL

To remove tar, use a rag to rub vegetable oil or shortening into the tar. Let it stand for a few moments and then rub it off.

WALL CUBBIES

To make custom wall cubbies for garden supplies or sports equipment, screw suitably sized galvanized buckets to the wall. Assemble the cubbies by first arranging the buckets. Next fasten the buckets together by drilling holes in the sides and bolting them to one another. Then drill holes through the bottoms of the buckets and attach them to the wall.

WHITEWALL TIRES, CLEANING

To clean whitewall tires, soak a rag in denatured alcohol mixed with a little hydrogen peroxide. Apply it to the sidewalls and let it penetrate for two minutes. Repeat the application and then rub the dirt off with another rag that has been dampened with the alcohol.

To remove curb marks, apply washing soda (available in the laundry section of stores) with a wet brush and then rinse.

WINDSHIELD, CLEANING

To clean bugs off of the car windshield and wiper blades, sprinkle dry baking soda on a damp sponge and scrub. Rinse and polish.

WINDSHIELD, DE-ICING

Keep a small container of kitchen salt in your car during the winter in case your windshield becomes coated with ice. To remove the ice, rub a handful of salt over the windshield.

WINDSHIELD WIPERS, CLEANING

Sprinkle dry baking soda on a damp sponge to clean grease and dirt from windshield wipers.

Before replacing wipers that are not working properly, try rubbing the blades with sandpaper to clean and smooth them.

CLOSETS AND STORAGE

CEDAR

Cedar smells great and protects your clothes from moths and carpet beetles. To make a cedar-lined closet, nail pieces of cedar right onto the walls. Or paint your closet with cedar oil (available at most hardware stores). There's also a range of cedar products such as hangers, hooks and balls, and liners for drawers, garment bags, and boxes.

To refresh an old cedar closet or chest, sand the boards.

HANGER BRAKES

Wrap a rubber band tightly around the end of the hook on a hanger to stop it from falling off the closet rod. The rubber will act as a brake if the hanger starts to slip.

HANGER SPACERS

If your clothes are getting pushed together and wrinkled while hanging in a closet, try replacing the hanger rod with a piece of chain. Hook the hangers into the links, and the chain will keep your clothes separated. *See illustration next page*

To keep hangers from bunching up on a wooden clothes rod, put rubber-headed tacks about an inch apart on top of the rod.

HOOK PROTECTORS

To prevent coat hooks from damaging your clothes, skewer small sponge-rubber balls on the hooks.

MOISTURE

To reduce dampness in a closet or storage area, tie six to 12 pieces of chalk in a bundle. Hang the bundle in the closet. The chalk will absorb moisture.

ODOR

If you keep a laundry basket in your closet, sprinkle baking soda in the bottom to keep it smelling fresh.

To keep seldom-used items smelling fresh (such as guest towels or sheets), store them in plastic containers with scented dryer sheets.

If your clothes smell of mildew, hang them outdoors to air out. Then mix 1 cup baking soda into a bucket of hot water and scrub the closet. Or place a pan of water and ammonia in the closet overnight.

Another way to get rid of musty smells is to put charcoal briquettes (the type without lighter fluid) in the closet. Close the door and leave them there overnight.

PEST CONTROL

If you're using mothballs, hang them as high as possible in closets. The fumes move downward.

If you don't want your clothes smelling like mothballs, use a natural solution that smells great: Mix one-fourth cup whole cloves with one-fourth cup black peppercorns. Add several small pieces of cinnamon sticks, and wrap the mix in cheesecloth. Hang the bundle in your closet or storage area. This will repel moths.

Silverfish feed on the starch in book or magazine bindings, wallpaper glue, and starched clothing. To repel silverfish, sprinkle a little cinnamon spice in the corners of your closets and drawers.

After boxing items for storage, tape the edges and seams of the box to keep silverfish and spiders out.

WARPED DOORS

If a closet door is warped, apply heat from a heat lamp to the convex side. Don't hold the lamp too close, or it might damage the door's finish. Remove the heat once the warp disappears. Coat both sides and edges with sealer to prevent further warping.

Doors and Windows

BAMBOO BLINDS

Use a strong solution of saltwater to clean bamboo blinds. The saltwater also helps the blinds maintain their shape.

To prevent mildew, paint a thin coat of clear shellac on the blinds. At the same time, dip the knots at the end of the cord into the shellac; it will prevent the knots from untying.

CURTAIN ROD, BROKEN

You can temporarily repair a split curtain rod (the sliding type) using coat hanger wire. Bend a piece of the wire into a "hairpin" shape about 15 inches long and spring it into the slots.

DOOR, BANGING

If a storm or screen door bangs shut, silence it with foam weather stripping. Use the type of weather stripping with peel-off adhesive backing, and attach a few pieces to the frame against which the door shuts. The door will still close completely, but it will do so quietly.

DOOR, SQUEAKY

To silence a squeaky door, spray some WD-40® on the door hinges. Open and close the door a few times. If that doesn't work, pull the pins out of the door hinges and rub them with petroleum jelly. Replace the pins, and you should have a quiet door. *See illustration*

DOOR, STICKING

If a door sticks when it's shut, tape a strip of medium-grit sandpaper on the area where it sticks to the frame. The action of opening and closing the door will smooth off the high spots.

If you can't tell where the door sticks, rub a piece of chalk on the edge of the door and close it. Open the door and tape the sandpaper on the area that's missing the chalk.

DOOR HINGES, SAGGING

If a door sags because of loose hinge screws, remove the screws and fill the worn holes with twisted steel wool. Then replace the screws. It's a quick fix that should hold for a long time.

DOOR HINGES, SQUEAKY

If an interior door squeaks, take the hinge pins out one at a time and rub a No. 2 pencil over the pin. Replace the pins, and your door should open and close silently.

DOOR LOCKS

Use a silicone spray in your locks to keep them working smoothly. You can also spray the key itself and insert it into the lock, instead of oiling the lock.

You also can use a No. 2 pencil to lubricate door locks. Simply rub both sides of your house key with the pencil, and then work the key into the lock.

If your door lock rattles, first check to make sure all the screws are tight. If that's not the problem, check the strike plate for a small tab inside the latch hole. Bend this tab out slightly and close the door to see if the rattle is gone. You may need to try this a few times – bending the tab only slightly each time – before the rattle is completely gone.

DOOR, WARPED

Use an ordinary heat lamp to straighten a warped door. Hold the lamp close to the convex side of the door until the warp disappears (be careful not to hold it too close, or you'll damage the finish on the door). Then apply a sealer to the sides and edges of the door to keep moisture out.

FRAMES, ALUMINUM

To preserve the bright finish, coat aluminum door and window frames annually with silicone (sold in auto supply stores). Also wipe some of the silicone into the window channels to make them slide easily in cold weather.

To prevent aluminum frames from pitting, wipe them twice a year with a soft cloth dipped in kerosene.

GLASS, CLEANING

Avoid washing windows on sunny days. They'll dry too fast and leave streaks.

To get windows sparkling clean, add a half-cup cornstarch to a bucket of warm water. Buff dry with a lint-free cloth or paper towel. The cornstarch will leave a natural shine on the window.

Pour leftover liquid tea (any kind) into a spray bottle and use it for day-to-day window cleaning. It works great on everything from finger smudges to dust.

Don't use newspaper to clean your windows. It might help you get streak-free glass, but it also will leave hard-to-remove marks on your paint and trim. Use cheap paper towels or a lint-free cloth instead.

Use up-and-down strokes to clean the inside of the glass and left-to-right strokes to clean the outside. If there's a streak, you'll know which side to clean.

GLASS, CRACKED

To temporarily fix a cracked window, paint the crack with a coat of white shellac. It won't obscure the view, and it will keep the weather out until you can replace the glass.

GLASS, FROSTED

To prevent frost from forming on your windows during the winter months, rub the outside of the glass with alcohol or salt water. Then buff with a soft cloth.

GLASS, SCRATCHED

If you notice minor scratches in glass, polish them out using a soft cloth and extra-whitening toothpaste.

HINGES, INSTALLING

When installing surface-mounted hinges, first tape them into place. Use masking tape to cover the hinge, and overlap both ends by about an inch. Make some starter holes (going through the tape), and then drive in the screws. When you're done, just peel off the tape.

See illustration next page

PEST CONTROL

Cleaning window and door screens with kerosene will keep mosquitoes from settling on them.

To keep insects from entering your home, caulk around doors and windows (inside and out) to fill cracks and crevices. Use a quality silicone or acrylic latex caulk (you can paint the latex caulk).

Seal gaps under sliding glass doors by lining the bottom track with foam weather stripping.

SCREENS, CLEANING

Use a handheld vacuum with a brush attachment to clean your door and window screens. If you don't have one, use a scrap of carpeting as a brush or roll a rough, dry paint roller over the screens.

SCREENS, PRIVACY

To add privacy to a bathroom window screen or sleeping porch, paint the screens with aluminum paint. You'll be able to see out, but people won't be able to see in. White paint thinned with turpentine also works well.

SCREENS, REPAIR

Use dabs of clear nail polish or modeling glue to repair holes less than a half inch across. Dab the hole a few times, then wait for the polish or glue to dry. Repeat this process until the hole is sealed.

SHADES

Use a soft eraser to remove spots and stains from a window shade.

Cover a shade with wallpaper to give it a new look or a decorative pattern or color.

Use a small suction cup to keep the shade from blowing if the window is open. Attach the suction cup to the pull string or bottom edge of the shade.

WINDOWS, STICKING

If a window is sticking, run a pizza cutter along the groove. It will loosen a frame that's been painted shut or is swollen because of humidity. **_See illustration_**

If the window is still sticking, rub a candle or a bar of soap along the inside of the vertical tracks. This will lubricate the track, decreasing the friction and making it easier to open and close the window. This technique also works with sliding glass doors.

ELECTRICAL

APPLIANCE FAILURE

If an appliance is not working, unplug it and check the socket by plugging in another appliance that you know is working. If the socket doesn't work, check the main fuse box.

If an appliance repeatedly blows a fuse, trips the circuit breaker, or shocks you, unplug and replace it or have it fixed by a professional.

COMPUTERS

Use a voltage surge suppressor to protect your computer against hardware damage or loss of data from electrical surges.

Unplug your computer directly from the wall outlet during all electrical storms. A surge suppressor will not protect the computer from a lightning strike.

If there's a blackout while you're working on your computer, turn the computer off. When the power comes back on, a voltage spike could damage your equipment.

ELECTRIC BLANKETS

When in use, electric blankets should be flat on the bed (no folds or creases).

Store blankets in a dry area and do not put anything on top of them. Roll the blankets up instead of folding them to avoid creasing the thermostats inside.

Do not use pins to secure an electric blanket; they can damage the wiring.

Wash blankets according to the manufacturer's instructions. Do not dry-clean electric blankets because the solvents can damage the insulation in the wires.

ELECTRIC CORD, SAFETY

Make sure all of your cords are in good condition and placed out of traffic areas.

Never nail or staple cords to walls, baseboards, or other objects.

Do not run cords under carpets or rugs, or allow furniture on them.

Keep cords away from heat, water, and grease.

Never handle cords with wet hands.

Remove a cord from a socket by pulling on the plug, not the cord itself.

Never use a cord that feels hot.

ELECTRIC CORD, STORAGE

To store extension cords, coil the cord and then store it inside an old toilet tissue tube. **See illustration**

ELECTRIC FANS, MAINTENANCE

After you've oiled an electric fan, cover it with a large paper bag. Run the fan at top speed for three minutes, and then remove the bag. The excess oil will be on the bag, not your furnishings.

ELECTRICAL OUTAGES

Keep a kit for electrical outages near the fuse box. This kit should contain a flashlight with working batteries, a selection of fuses and fuse wires, a screwdriver, candles, and matches.

Label all circuits to make it easier to isolate the one that's not working.

EXTENSION CORD, SAFETY

Unwind an extension cord completely before each use. The cord can generate heat if it's used while bundled.

Use extension cords as temporary fixes, not as permanent wiring.

Be careful not to overload an extension cord; use one extension cord per appliance. If you overload the cord's capacity, it can overheat, melt, and cause a fire.

Unplug an extension cord that's not in use. The cord will conduct electricity until it's unplugged from the outlet.

HALOGEN LIGHTS

Halogen desk and floor lamps are fire hazards. Replace them.

LIGHT BULB, BROKEN

If a light bulb has broken off in the socket, first turn the power off. Then take a bar of soap and press it over the broken ends and twist counter clockwise to remove the remainder of the bulb. You can also use half of a potato, modeling clay, or a cork.

See illustration opposite

If there is broken glass on a counter or floor, swab the area with wet, absorbent cotton. The glass shards will stick to the cotton.

To keep a bulb from breaking off in the socket again, apply a thin film of petroleum jelly around the base of the new bulb before putting it into the socket.

LIGHT BULB, DUST
A layer of dust will impair the quality of light provided by a bulb. Dust exposed light bulbs often.

LIGHT BULB, NOT WORKING
To fix a new bulb that's not making contact in the socket, first remove the bulb. Then pry up one edge of

the contact plate on the bulb.

LIGHT SWITCHES
To make it easy to find light switches in the dark, paint the tips of your light switches with glow-in-the-dark paint. The paint will dry clear, making it invisible during the day. After the lights have been turned off, the paint will glow for approximately eight hours.

OUTLETS, DRAFTS
If you feel a draft coming though the outlets in an outside wall, install outlet insulation covers (available in the weather-stripping section of hardware or home improvement stores).

OUTLETS, SAFETY
Loose-fitting plugs can overheat and cause a fire. Do annual checks for outlets that have loose-fitting plugs. Replace any missing or broken wall plates.

Install safety covers on all outlets that are accessible to children.

POWER OUTAGE
If you've lost power, first check to see if other homes in the neighborhood have lost power. If not, go to your breaker box. If one of the breakers has been tripped, it will be in the center position. Flip it to the "off" position, and then back to the "on" position. If the breaker will not stay in the on position, it may be faulty. Call an electrician.

If you've lost power in one area of the house, check the outlets that have a ground fault circuit interrupter (GFCI). GFCIs are normally found in areas where water might be, such as the kitchen and bathrooms, and are designed to protect people from electric shocks. This type of outlet will have buttons on it to trip and reset the power. Try pressing the reset button to restore power to the related locations.

UTILITIES

Label the switches at the main so it's easy to know which direction is "off."

Exterior

CAULKING

Take a walk around your house each fall with a caulking gun and fill any holes and cracks. Look for openings around pipes, windows, door frames, and areas where siding materials meet.

Keep a dryer sheet handy when you're applying caulk. The sheet has a lubricant that will help smooth out the caulk.

DOORMATS

Use a handsaw to cut a piece of plastic suspended ceiling grid to fit under your doormats. This will raise the doormats slightly, increasing the air circulation and preventing them from becoming soggy.

DRAINAGE

Make sure the grading around the foundation of your house is adequate and that the downspouts are dumping water sufficiently away from the house. Use splash blocks or a drainage system.

DRIVEWAY, OIL STAINS

Sprinkle new oil spots on a concrete driveway with kitty litter. After the litter absorbs the oil, sweep the area clean. Next, scrub the stain with liquid dish soap and water. You may have to scrub the area several times before the oil is completely gone. (Use a nylon bristle scrubbing brush. A wire brush might scratch the concrete finish and leave a permanent scar.)

FOUNDATION

Once a year, check your foundation for cracks and blocked vents. Repair any cracks with ready-mix cement or heavy caulking material.

Trim trees and shrubs so that they're not touching the foundation, exterior walls, or roof of your house.

GUTTERS

Each spring and fall, make sure your gutters and downspouts are free of debris (leaves, sticks, etc.) that will block the flow of water from your roof.

Instead of climbing on a ladder to inspect gutters for debris and damage, tape a small mirror to the end of a rake or other long-handled tool. *See illustration opposite*

Discoloration at the top, outside rim of the gutter is a sign that there is buildup in the gutter, and that water is draining poorly and overflowing.

GUTTERS AND DOWNSPOUTS, CLEANING

Clean gutters when they're dry. Use gloves to dig out the gunk, or make a scoop by cutting the bottom out of a half-gallon plastic milk jug or a soda bottle.

Use an old pair of metal barbecue tongs to lift out bulky items. After gutters are clear of debris, use a garden hose to flush them out.

Make sure downspouts direct water away from the house. If needed, add splash blocks or extend the downspouts.

After you clean the gutters and downspouts, wash the exterior of the house with a garden hose and mild detergent. (Beware of using a pressure washer on siding because it can force water under the siding, causing mildew and rot.)

MICE

Mice often enter a house through a connected garage because the garage door is not sealed well. Put catch-and-release traps on each side of the garage door (on the inside of the garage), and check them daily. Release mice far from your home.

Attach tight-fitting weather stripping on the bottom of all exterior doors, including the garage. Mice can fit under a door that is only three-eighths of an inch off the ground.

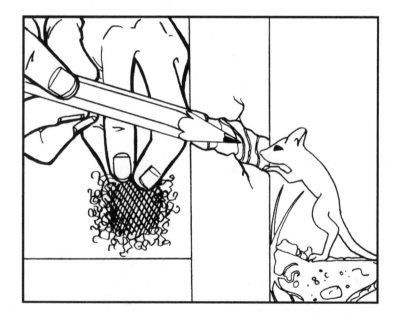

Check for holes in the walls of your house and garage. If you can fit a pencil through the hole, it's big enough for a mouse to get through.

Temporarily plug holes in the wall with steel wool. Use wire mesh and expanding foam for more permanent results. The mesh will stop the rodent if it tries to chew through the foam. *See illustration opposite*

MILDEW

Apply bleach to an old sponge and use it to scrub mildew spots from the exterior of your house.

ROOF

To check the roof for leaks, inspect the underside of the roof from the attic. If you spot signs of water damage, call a professional.

Use a ladder and binoculars to check the roof for damaged or loose shingles, gaps where the roofing and siding meet vents and flues, and damaged mortar around a chimney.

If you have to get on your roof, crawl around on your hands and knees instead of walking. Put tools in a container that won't slide, and keep the container above you so you don't step on it and loose your balance.

Never climb a ladder when you're the only one home.

WINDOW WELLS

Use a leaf rake to scoop up any debris that has collected in window wells. Leaves, newspapers, and other windblown trash trapped in window wells can hold moisture and foster mold growth.

FLOORS

CARPET, CLEANING
The best way to clean carpets is by frequent and thorough vacuuming. Have carpets professionally cleaned at least once a year, or more if you live with a smoker or have pets or heavy traffic.

CARPET, STAINS
Blot liquid stains using a white, absorbent towel or napkin as soon as possible.

Scrape up solid or semi-solid stains with a spoon or spatula. Then vacuum up as much as possible.

Do not scrub or brush a stain; it can harm the fibers and set the stain.

Pretest all spot removers on a hidden area of the carpet.

CARPET, WAX REMOVAL
To remove wax that has dripped on a carpet, place a clean, damp white cloth over the wax. Next put a hot iron over the cloth. The steam will reach into the carpet fibers and melt the wax onto the cloth. You may need to repeat this a few times to completely remove the wax. *See illustration next page*

CARPET, PET STAINS

Blot up as much of the moisture as possible with a clean white cloth or towel. Treat the area with a mild detergent, rinse with water, and neutralize the odor with a solution of 1 tablespoon ammonia and a half a cup of water to neutralize the odor. Spray the solution on the affected area and then blot it up. Blot up all excess moisture and put a fan nearby to help dry the area.

CARPET, PIN REMOVAL

To find pins that have been dropped onto a carpet or plush rug, shine a flashlight beam over the floor. The pins will reflect the light and be easier to find. Use a small magnet to pick them up.

CARPET, GREASE STAINS

Rub dry baking soda into the area that has the grease. Let it stand for a few hours and then vacuum.

FLEA EXTERMINATION

To get rid of fleas, apply cedar oil to pieces of wrapping paper and place them around the house, including underneath the beds.

HARDWOOD, CLEANING

Brew a pot of strong tea, let it cool to room temperature, and use it to wash your hardwood floors. Any tea is OK; it's the tannic acid that cleans and leaves a beautiful shine. Be careful, however, because it also leaves the floors a bit slippery. *See illustration*

HARDWOOD, SCRATCHES

Use a hair dryer to heat a crayon that's close in color to the floor and draw over the scratch marks. You may need to buff and reapply the crayon a few times.

If the hardwood is walnut or pecan, use the oil in the corresponding nut to cover the scratch. Crack the nut and rub it over the scratch. Buff and reapply if needed.

LINOLEUM, PAINT-STAINED

First try to remove oil-based paint with turpentine or mineral spirits. If that doesn't work, rub the paint spots gently with fine steel wool and then wax and polish the area.

LINOLEUM, SMALL HOLES

To patch small holes in linoleum, make a thick paste of finely chopped cork and shellac. Wait for the paste to harden and then sandpaper it smooth. Touch it up with matching paint.

ROACH EXTERMINATION

Save and dry chrysanthemum blooms; they contain a poison that's deadly to roaches. Crush the blooms and sprinkle in areas where roaches are found.

THROW RUGS, CLEANING

Use the bathtub to wash throw rugs that won't fit into the washing machine. Add laundry detergent and use a broom to scrub the rugs or a clean sink plunger to get the dirt out.

Mix a little starch in the rinse water to make the rug less likely to curl on the floor.

THROW RUGS, SLIDING
Put an old rubber bathmat under a rug to keep it from sliding.

VINYL FLOOR, REPLACING TILES
If you need to replace a damaged tile but don't have extras from when the tile was installed, check under appliances and cabinets to see if there are any you can use.

To remove a damaged tile, heat it using a hair dryer. Carefully remove the tile using a wide putty knife, being careful not to damage neighboring tiles. Remove the old adhesive using a paint scraper. Spread the new adhesive with a small, notched trowel. Set the new tile in place. Press down on the tile and then wipe off any adhesive that comes up through the cracks.

The tile will need to be weighted for about 24 hours. To do this, first put waxed paper down and then add books, bricks, or whatever you can find that's heavy.

See illustration next page

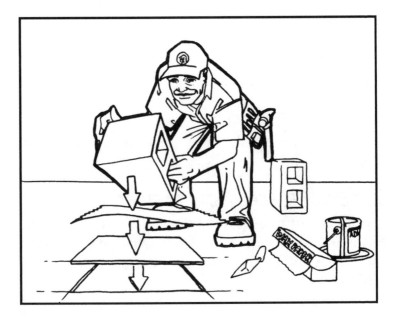

VINYL FLOOR, TEARS AND GOUGES

Use clear nail polish to fill gouges. It may take several layers to build up the gouge. You can also use clear nail polish to "glue" a tear down. Put several more layers of polish over the tear to waterproof the surface.

FURNISHINGS

BED SLATS, LOOSE

To anchor loose bed slats that are threatening to fall out, wrap rubber bands around the ends of the slats where they would go into the bed rails.

BED, SQUEAKING

Pour a little melted paraffin wax into the joints and corners of a wooden bed frame to silence squeaks. The hardened wax acts as a lubricant.

BOOKEND, SLIDING

Glue wide rubber bands to the bottom of a bookend to stop it from sliding. *See illustration next page*

BOTTLES, DECORATIVE

To remove the neck of a glass bottle, soak a piece of twine in paraffin wax. Tie the twine around the bottle where you want the break to be. Set fire to the twine. Once it has burned, pour cold water on the twine, and the bottle will break cleanly in that spot.

CANDLE, DRIP PREVENTION

Put salt around the top of a candle to prevent it from dripping.

CANDLE, PERFUMED
Customize the scent of an unscented candle by lightly spraying it with perfume or cologne. When the candle burns, it will give off that scent.

CANDLE, PRESERVATION
Once a candle has burned down a little, insert a tea candle so the larger candle will last longer.

CANDLE, STRAIGHTENING
To correct a bent candle, put it in a dish of hot water until it softens. Straighten it out and run it under cold water to set the wax.

CANDLE, STUCK

If votive candles are stuck in the candleholders, put them in the freezer overnight. The candles should pop right out in the morning.

CANDLE, TIGHT FIT

To fit a slightly large candle into a candleholder, dip the end of the candle in hot water. This will make the wax soft enough to squeeze it into the holder.

CURTAINS AND DRAPERY, CLEANING

Put curtains in the clothes dryer with a tennis ball to dust and freshen them. Run the dryer on the "air" setting for 20 to 30 minutes.

Use the dust attachment on your vacuum cleaner to remove dust from curtains. Work from top to bottom. To remove fold lines from a new set of cotton curtains, hang them and spray the lines with water. As the water dries, the weight of the curtain will pull out the folds.

CUSHION FILLER

To enhance the filling in an old cushion, cut up large plastic bags and stuff them into the cushion.

DENT REMOVAL, WOOD

Remove a small dent from wood with a damp cloth (preferably terry cloth), a bottle cap, and a clothes iron that is preheated to the cotton setting. Put the cloth over the dent and position the bottle cap, teeth down, on the cloth directly over the dent. Set the iron on the bottle cap and press it gently into the cloth. As the iron heats the bottle cap, steam will build under the cap, raising the grain of the wood. You may have to repeat the process a few times to completely remove the dent. *See illustration*

DRAWER PULLS, CHILDREN'S

Swap out the drawer pulls on a child's dresser with alphabet letter blocks. Use long wood screws to attach the blocks from the inside. To help the child organize, use the letters for the clothes that are in a particular drawer.

DRAWER PULLS, LOOSE

To fix a screw-type drawer pull that has become loose, remove the screw and dip it in glue. Replace the screw after the glue has dried.

DRAWER, STICKING

Apply wax to the surfaces of wooden drawer guides that stick.

DRAWERS, SLIDING

Press thumbtacks into the runners of drawers that are difficult to open or close.

FURNITURE, SCRATCHED

To hide scratches on dark wood furniture, dip a cotton ball in iodine and dab it on the scratch. After it has dried, rub the scratch with furniture polish.

FURNITURE, BROKEN SCREWS

If a wood screw breaks off below the surface of the wood, do not try to remove it. Instead, drive the screw in deeper, use wood filler to plug the hole, and start a new screw.

FURNITURE, MOVING

To move furniture, first invest in some specially made furniture glides. Place them under furniture legs or heavy appliances and then slide the objects with ease. The glides will reduce the risk of injury to flooring, furniture, and you.

GILT FRAMES, CLEANING

To clean gilt picture frames, rub them with a small sponge that has been dipped in oil of turpentine. The oil will evaporate quickly.

KNOB, TIGHTENING

To tighten a loose knob or cabinet pull, remove the screw, bend it slightly, and replace.

LAMPSHADES, DUST REMOVAL

To clean a lampshade, gently vacuum it with one of the brush attachments of a vacuum cleaner. Or brush it with a clean paintbrush while blowing the dust away with a blow dryer on the cool setting.

LEATHER CARE

Clean leather furniture once a year with mild soap and water. Once the piece is dry, apply leather conditioner and wipe with a clean cloth so there is no residue.

NICKEL-PLATE AND CHROME, POLISHING

To polish nickel-plate and chrome, dip a damp cloth in cornstarch and buff the surface. When dry, polish with a soft, clean cloth.

PAINTINGS, CLEANING

Have valuable paintings cleaned by a professional. To clean a purely decorative painting, dip a rag in luke-warm, mild soapy water and clean one small area at a time. Dry each area as soon as you have cleaned it. Once the entire painting has been cleaned and dried, wipe it with a flannel cloth moistened with linseed oil.

PET FUR, REMOVAL
To remove dog or cat fur from drapes and upholstery, put on a pair of rubber gloves and run your hands over the fur. It should come right off.

PIANO KEYS, CLEANING
Dip a clean cloth in milk and use it to clean and polish piano keys. Or squirt some white toothpaste on a wet cloth and rub the keys clean. After either technique, buff with a soft, dry cloth.

PICTURE FRAMES, ANTIQUING
Rub chalk over the wooden frame. Lightly dust the frame so there isn't too much chalk. Go over the entire frame with brown shoe polish.

PICTURES, HANGING
To protect the walls, push thumbtacks into the back corners of picture frames. When the picture is hung, or bumped accidentally, the tacks will protect the wall from getting scratched.

POTTERY, REPAIR
To repair a broken dish or handle, fill a wide container with six inches of sand. The sand will hold the pieces in place while you make the repair. Wipe the exposed edges with a soft brush to remove dust. Apply a thin, even layer of epoxy glue to all the surfaces you will be gluing. Firmly press the broken

pieces together. Use rubber bands or masking tape to hold the pieces together while the glue dries.

See illustration

SCREWS, LOOSE

Remove the screw from the area where it is loose. Wrap the screw with tape and reinsert into the original screw hole.

SHEETS

To keep all the pieces of a sheet set together, fold them as usual and slip the entire bundle into one of the pillowcases. It will also keep your linen closet in order.

TABLE, PAPER REMOVAL

To remove paper that has become stuck to a wooden table, saturate the paper with furniture oil. Let it soak in and then rub it with a soft cloth to remove the paper.

UPHOLSTERY, CLEANING

Use the brush attachment of a vacuum to remove dust and debris from upholstery. To remove stains, add a little water to a mild detergent and use an eggbeater to whip up thick, dry suds. Brush the dry suds on the stains, one area at time. Wipe the suds off immediately with a damp cloth.

UPHOLSTERY, RIPS

To repair a small rip in upholstery, apply adhesive tape from the backside of the tear, sticky side up. Pull the torn edges together, tucking the raveled threads under, and press down on the tape.

VASE, CLEANING

To clean narrow-necked bottles or vases, cut a lemon into small pieces and put the pieces into the bottle with some uncooked rice. Add water and shake until the bottle is clean. Rinse with warm water.

WASTEBASKETS, METAL

Wax both sides of metal wastebaskets to prevent them from rusting. The wax will also prevent dust from accumulating and make the wastebaskets easier to clean.

WICKER

To dust a wicker chair, use a clean paintbrush. The paint bristles will reach into crevices that a dust rag would miss.

GENERAL

CERAMIC TILE, REPAIR
Use automobile paint to camouflage a chip in ceramic tile. There are many colors that can be blended to match your tile. Apply a liberal amount of paint to the chipped area and allow it to dry.

CLOCK, NOISY
To quiet an electric clock that vibrates from worn bearings, set it on a thin pad of foam rubber.

COMPUTER KEYBOARDS, CLEANING
Use a pencil eraser to clean individual keys on a computer keyboard. Then dust using a crafter's stenciling brush.

DECALS, REMOVAL
To remove decals, first paint them with a few coats of hot vinegar. Let the vinegar soak in, and then wash the decal off.

DESK DRAWERS, CLEANING
To clean desk or junk drawers without picking up all the little paperclips, staples, or pins, slip a piece of pantyhose over the end of the vacuum nozzle.

ENVELOPE SEALER
To wet the glue on envelopes, wrap an ice cube in a

thin, clean cloth. It should melt just fast enough to keep the cloth sufficiently damp to seal a stack of envelopes. *See illustration*

FLOWERS, FRESH

Add a little hydrogen peroxide to the water when filling a vase with fresh flowers. It will extend the life of the flowers by preventing flower-killing bacteria from taking hold.

Or add a piece of charcoal to the water. The flowers will last longer and the water will not smell moldy.

To keep a flower arrangement in place, use a flat

shower drain replacement at the top of the vase. Slide the flower stems through the grate holes.

GLUE, CAPS
To prevent the cap from sticking on a tube of glue, rub the threads inside the cap with a little petroleum jelly.

GOLF CLUBS
Use aluminum foil to clean golf clubs. Crumple a sheet into a ball, dip it in water, and rub it on the clubs.

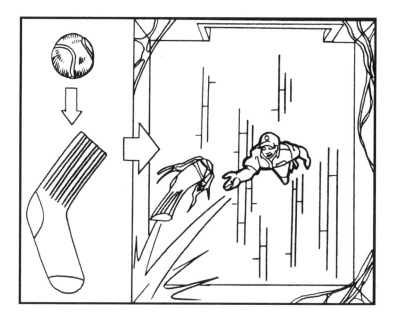

HARD-TO-REACH AREAS, CLEANING
Tape a feather duster to a yardstick or broom handle

to reach long narrow spots, such as between the refrigerator and a counter.

To remove cobwebs from a vaulted ceiling, put a tennis ball in a sock and gently toss it at the cobwebs. It may take a few tries, but you'll be able to knock down the cobwebs. **See illustration previous page**

Dip a cotton swab in glass cleaner to get corners and crevices clean.

HIGH CHAIRS, CLEANING

To wash really messy high chairs or other bulky items, clean them in the shower. The mess will go down the drain and it will be easier to rinse them thoroughly.

IRON, BROWN SPOTS

Remove brown spots from a clothes iron by dipping fine steel wool in warm vinegar and gently scrubbing the surface.

MATCHES, WATERPROOFING

To waterproof matches, dip the top half in clear nail polish. This also makes the matches burn better in strong breezes.

PLANTS, WATERING

To make plants healthier, water them with room-temperature rainwater, flat club soda, or the leftover water from cooking pasta.

PRICE TAG, REMOVAL

To remove remnants of price tags or the glue they leave behind on a new item, rub the sticky area with peanut butter. Let it sit for a few minutes, and then scrub it off with soapy water and a sponge.

SHOES, ODOR REMOVAL

To eliminate odors from foul-smelling shoes, fill the toe of an old sock with baking soda and slip it into the shoes when they're not being worn.

SKI GOGGLES, ANTI-FOG

Use foam shaving cream to clean ski goggles. It not only cleans them, but it also adds an anti-fog coating on the surface. *See illustration*

SPLINTER REMOVAL

To remove a splinter, cover the area with white wood glue. Wait for the glue to dry and then peel it off with tweezers. The splinter should come out with the glue. Repeat if needed.

STAPLER, REFILL INDICATOR

Paint a dab of red nail polish near the end of each bar of staples so that you'll know when it's time to refill the stapler.

HEATING AND COOLING

AIR CONDITIONER, COMPRESSOR

If the outside compressor is dirty, first disconnect the power to the unit. Then use a garden hose to spray it clean.

If there is a power outage or if you've accidentally turned off your air conditioner, wait at least six minutes before restarting it. This will prevent damage to the compressor.

Keep the compressor covered during the winter. If you have window units, remove them each fall.

AIR CONDITIONER, FILTERS

Clogged, dirty filters will block airflow and cut your air conditioner's efficiency. You'll save money by cleaning or replacing your air conditioning system's filter(s) once a month during the cooling season.

Check the area around your unit for sources of dust and debris that will reduce airflow around the condenser (dryer vents, lawn mowers and falling leaves are common culprits). Trim trees and bushes so that they are at least two feet from the unit.

See illustration next page

AIR CONDITIONER, LEAKING WATER

Periodically check the drain line for leaking water (a sign that it's clogged and could be causing water damage inside the house). To prevent clogs, pour a cup of bleach into the line from the inside. To remove an existing clog, remove the paper filter, attach a wet/dry vacuum to the drain line outside, and suck the clog out.

AIR CONDITIONER, MAINTENANCE

Schedule an annual tune-up to maintain efficiency. As part of this checkup, the technician should use a high-pressure vacuum to clean the drain. This will prevent any backups that could cause mold growth in your air conditioner and water damage to the walls and ceilings.

CARBON MONOXIDE SAFETY

Install carbon monoxide detectors on every level of your home and in sleeping areas. Buy detectors that connect to a wall plug or electrical wiring system.

Ensure that gas appliances are properly adjusted and working according to the manufacturer's instructions. Operate them only in adequately ventilated areas.

Have your chimneys and flues cleaned regularly to remove soot deposits, leaves, animal nests, and other debris.

ENERGY CONSERVATION, GENERAL

In winter, set your heater between 66 and 68 degrees. For each degree you set your thermostat above 70 degrees, expect a 3 percent rise in energy costs.

Install a programmable thermostat to automatically lower the heat at night.

Use area rugs on cold floors. If your feet are cold, your body will feel cold.

Clean and vacuum refrigerator coils every six months.

Set the refrigerator temperature in the middle range, between 38 and 40 degrees.

Unplug all appliances that you store on counters and use periodically. They draw electricity when they are plugged in.

When using the clothes dryer, do multiple loads consecutively to take advantage of the heat that has built up in the dryer.

Insulate your water heater with an insulation blanket and insulate any exposed pipes.

Keep the water temperature on your water heater set at 120 degrees. If you use a dishwasher, set it at 140 degrees.

ENERGY CONSERVATION, SUMMER

Set your air conditioner to 78 degrees or higher.

Close windows and shades on the east side of the house early in the day (this will allow you to take advantage of the cool morning air on the shady sides of the house). As the sun moves overhead, close the windows on the other sides of the house. Leave them closed as long as it's warmer outside than it is inside.

Open windows at night for cross ventilation.

Plant leafy (deciduous) trees on the sunny side of your house. They'll provide shade during the summer, and in the winter they'll drop their leaves and let the warming sunshine through. *See illustration next page*

Use window or ceiling fans at night instead of air conditioning. Make sure your ceiling fans are blowing air downward in the summer.

Keep your windows closed when running the air conditioning.

FURNACE

Clean or replace filters once a month so the furnace runs efficiently and saves on heating costs.

Check your furnace's flame. It should be mostly blue and steady. If you see a pale yellow or wavy flame, your furnace is not working properly. Call a professional.

Keep combustible materials (papers, paint, rags, etc.) away from your furnaces (and water heaters, gas ranges and dryers).

Schedule an inspection and cleaning each fall to make sure your furnace is operating safely and efficiently.

GAS, SAFETY

Know how to turn your gas off at the main. If you're unsure about how to do this, ask a knowledgeable neighbor or the meter reader.

Keep your pilot lights lit. If you put them out to save energy, a dangerous gas buildup can occur.

Never block flues or vents in rooms with gas appliances.

Never use your gas range to heat your home.

INSULATION

Insulate the attic to prevent heat loss in the winter and heat gain in the summer. This will save on your heating and cooling costs.

Weather-strip and caulk around doors and windows to reduce heating and cooling costs.

See illustration next page

SPACE HEATERS, SAFETY

Space heaters can cause fires and injuries. Use them only as supplemental heat and unplug them when not in use.

Keep space heaters at least three feet from combustible materials such as bedding, clothes, drapes, furniture, or rugs.

Do not use space heaters in rooms where flammable liquids such as gas or kerosene are stored.

Don't use space heaters in rooms where children or pets can touch them.

UTILITIES

Label the switches at the mains for gas and water so it's easy to know which direction is "off."

KITCHEN

ALUMINUM PANS, CLEANING

To clean burnt-on food from an aluminum pan, boil water with half an onion in the pan for a few minutes. The burned substance will release and rise to the top.

BAKING SODA

Baking soda will stay good for three months in the freezer. After that, pour it down drains to keep them fresh.

BEATERS

To make beaters easier to clean, run them under cold water immediately after use. Use a toothbrush to clean tight spots. This also works for potato mashers.

BRASS

Dip half a lemon in salt and use it to clean brass.

BURNERS

To clean stove burners, simmer them in a pot of water with a little dish detergent.

CABINET PULLS

If the magnetic pulls on your cabinets are too strong, put a layer of tape over them. Add more tape until you're able to open the cabinets easily. If the magnets lose strength later, pull the tape off. *See illustration next page*

CAST-IRON SKILLET

To clean a cast-iron skillet, spray the outside with oven cleaner and let sit for two hours, and then use vinegar and water to remove the accumulated black stains.

After washing a cast-iron skillet, heat it on the stove until it's slightly hot, and then rub it with wax paper. The residue from the wax paper will prevent rust.

CHINA

To whiten discolored china, scrub it with baking soda or vinegar and salt.

Reuse plastic lids to protect china plates. Put a lid between plates when you're stacking them for storage.

CHROME
To polish chrome, use dry baking soda on a soft cloth.

To remove rust spots, rub them with aluminum foil and then wipe with a dry cloth. For extra cleaning power, first dip the aluminum in Coke® or Pepsi®.

COFFEEPOT
To clean a coffeepot, fill it with boiling water and add a teaspoon of baking soda. Rinse the pot with warm water. If there are still stains, scrub the pot with a mixture of equal parts salt and baking soda.

CUTTING BOARDS
Remove strong odors from a cutting board by rubbing it with half a lemon. Or scrub the board with baking soda.

To prevent the cutting board from slipping while you work, put a damp kitchen towel beneath it.

DISHWASHER
Freshen the dishwasher by pouring a cup of baking soda in the bottom and running the rinse cycle.

DOUBLE BOILERS

Put a few marbles in the bottom half of a double boiler. When they start to rattle, the water has boiled away.

DRAINS

Pour hot saltwater down your drains a couple of times a week to keep them free of grease and debris.

DRAINS, CLOGGED

See "Plumbing" section.

EGG SLICER

Use an egg slicer to cut strawberries and bananas for a fruit salad.

GARBAGE DISPOSAL, CLEANING

Clean the disposal with ice cubes and one-forth cup vinegar. If your disposal is really dirty, sprinkle one-third cup baking soda on top of the ice. When it sounds like the cubes are gone, run cold water. The water should back up until the ice melts, helping to wash the sides of the disposal.
See illustration next page

To freshen a foul-smelling disposal, drop in half a lemon.

GARBAGE DISPOSAL, CLOGGED

To loosen debris, toss a few ice cubes down the disposal, followed by an orange or lemon rind; then flush with cold water. Citrus is a natural degreaser.

GARBAGE DISPOSAL, NORMAL USE

Run cold water when you're using the garbage disposal. Hot water can melt fats in food, which will clog up the disposal and your pipes.

Do not overfill the disposal, and do not pour bleach, drain cleaners, or other chemicals into the disposal.

GARBAGE DISPOSAL, NOT WORKING

Check the motor for a reset button. Most garbage disposals have one.

GLASS, CHIPPED

To remove small chips from glassware, rub gently with fine sandpaper.

GLASS, CLEANING

To clean narrow-necked bottles or vases, cut a lemon into small pieces and put the pieces into the bottle with some uncooked rice. Add water and shake until the bottle is clean. Rinse with warm water.

To add extra sparkle to glass, add a little vinegar to the rinse water, and then polish with soft tissue paper.

GRATER

Before using a cheese or vegetable grater, coat it lightly with olive oil to make it easier to clean.

When it's time to clean the grater, scrub it with a vegetable brush or a clean toothbrush dipped in hot, soapy water. Rinse well and dry immediately.

GREASE FIRES

Keep baking soda near the stove in case of a grease fire. Use it to smother the fire.

GREASE SPATTERS

If grease spatters on clothing or wallpaper, sprinkle the stains immediately with cornstarch. This will make it easier to remove the stain later.

GREASY HANDS

To clean hands that are covered in grease or oil, rub them with a mixture of dishwashing soap and sugar.

ICE CUBES

Liven up ice cubes for drinks by adding fresh mint (great in iced tea), juice, fruit, or food coloring to the ice cube tray along with the water.

Use muffin tins as ice cube trays to get large cubes for packing coolers or adding to punch bowls.
See illustration next page

KETCHUP BOTTLE

If you're having trouble getting ketchup out of a new bottle, put a plastic straw into it. The straw will get air to the bottom and make it easier for the catsup to flow.

LAZY SUSANS

Increase storage space by making a Lazy Susan for a cabinet or shelf. Hammer a nail through the center of an aluminum or tin pie plate, and run it through two small washers under the plate.

MICROWAVE

Make cleaning the microwave easier by first putting a damp dish towel in it and setting the microwave on high for about a minute. The steam will loosen tough, crusty food spatters.

ODOR, REMOVAL

To neutralize fish odor in a frying pan, sprinkle salt into the pan, add hot water, and let it sit for a few minutes before washing.

To remove a burnt smell from the kitchen, boil water in an open pot with a cinnamon stick and half an apple.

To neutralize odors in garbage cans, pour cat litter

into an old pair of pantyhose and put it in the bottom of the can.

RUST SPOTS
To remove rust spots from pans, cut a potato in half. Sprinkle scouring powder on the pan, and then rub the rust spots with the potato.

SALTSHAKER
Add a little rice to a saltshaker to prevent clumps.

SCISSORS
Cut through sandpaper or steel wool several times to sharpen scissors. *See illustration*

SILVERWARE

Save the water used to boil potatoes and soak silverware in it to remove tarnish.

Use a piece of raw potato dipped in baking soda to clean extremely tarnished silverware.

SLIPPERY BOTTLES

Wrap wide rubber bands around slippery bottles to make them easier to grip.

SPONGES

Bacteria and microorganisms love kitchen sponges. Use cloth, paper towels, or disinfecting wipes instead.

If you do use a sponge, put it in the microwave on high for a minute before using it to clean dishes or wipe tables and counters. Throw it away after a few days.

SINKS, PORCELAIN

To remove stains, line the sink with paper towels. Saturate the towels with undiluted chlorine bleach and let them sit for about 30 minutes.

SINKS, STAINLESS STEEL

Use baking powder to clean the sink.

To remove stains that won't come out with baking power, mix three parts cream of tartar with one part hydrogen peroxide. Dab the mixture onto the stain using a damp cloth. Let it dry, and then wipe it clean with another damp cloth.

Minimize scratches on the sink by rubbing them with a cotton ball dipped in baby oil.

TEA KETTLE

Empty a tea kettle after each use to prevent sediment from collecting. Rinse the kettle with cold water before using it again.

THERMOS

To clean a thermos, soak it overnight in warm water mixed with a teaspoon of baking soda.

PAINTING AND STAINING

AGING TECHNIQUE
To make a surface look old, first apply a coat of wood glue. Let it dry for one to four hours. Next apply a coat of flat latex paint. The finish will crackle.

BRUSHES, MAINTENANCE
Use a hair comb to remove loose bristles from an old paintbrush.

After cleaning a paintbrush, close the bristles in a large spring clamp to keep them in shape. Then hang the clamp on a hook until the brush is dry.

To restore hard, dry paintbrushes, soak them in warm water with a little lye in it.

To remove old paint from a brush, simmer it in full-strength vinegar until the paint softens. Remove the old paint with a wire comb or brush. Then wash the brush in warm, soapy water.

Keep your paintbrushes soft and flexible for future use by adding a splash of fabric softener to the final rinse water.

CEILINGS
When using a paintbrush to paint a ceiling, first push the handle through an X cut into a paper plate. It will

help prevent the paint from dripping down the brush handle. *See illustration*

Use old bread bags or newspaper bags to protect the blades on your ceiling fan from spatters and drips while you're painting the ceiling.

FLOWERPOTS
To paint a flowerpot, place it upside down on a tin can. You'll be able to paint without having to touch the pot.

HINGES AND KNOBS
Before you start to paint a door, rub petroleum jelly

on the hinges and doorknobs. If you get paint on them, it will wipe off easily after the rest of the paint has dried.

LATEX OR OIL-BASED PAINT?

Before painting over an existing color, you'll need to determine what type of paint is already on the walls. Clean a small area with detergent and water. Rinse with water and dry the area completely. Next soak a cotton ball in alcohol and rub it over the cleaned area. Latex paint will come off on the cotton ball; oil-based paint will not.

If you have latex paint, you can paint over it with the same. If you have oil-based paint, you'll need to use an oil primer before you paint.

MESS, PREVENTION

Create an inexpensive liner by putting a paint tray inside a plastic grocery bag. When you're done painting, simply throw the bag away. Your tray stays as good as new.

Put your hand in a plastic bag before removing a roller cover to save your hand from getting covered with paint.

Eliminate splatters when you hammer the lid back on a paint can by first covering the lid with a plastic grocery bag.

METAL

If you paint galvanized metal without pre-treating it, your hard work will likely peel off. Rub full-strength white vinegar on the metal with a soft cloth and let it sit. After an hour, rinse the metal with water. When it's thoroughly dry, you can paint.

MIXING

Paint is not mixed exactly the same in each can. If you need more than one can to paint a room, blend the cans together so that the color change isn't noticeable. Once your first can of paint is half empty, add paint from the second can and stir. Add paint from the third can to the second and so on. This will balance the color variation.

Store a can of paint upside down for a few days before painting. This will make it easier to mix the paint.

To mix paint, pour it back and forth from the can to a bucket.

ODORS

To prevent odor, add about an ounce of vanilla extract to each gallon of paint. Stir well.

To remove the paint smell from a freshly painted room, cut a large onion in half and leave it in the room overnight. If you don't have an onion, add a teaspoon of ammonia to a pan of water and leave the pan in the room overnight.

OUTDOOR PAINTING

When painting a porch or outdoor stairs, stir sand into each can of paint. This will add traction, making the painted surface safer during wet weather.

To prevent insects from landing on wet paint during outdoor painting projects, stir several drops of citronella oil into the paint. It will repel bugs while the paint dries.

PAINT CANS

If you're painting directly from the paint can, wrap a heavy rubber band lengthwise around the can. This creates an edge on which to wipe excess paint off the brush and allows you to keep the can's edges clean for resealing. *See illustration*

Attach a paper plate to the bottom of the paint can before you start to paint. It will catch drips and make a handy spot to rest your paintbrush.

PAINT REMOVAL

Rub your hands with cooking oil and then wash with soap and warm water to remove paint. It's easier on your skin than paint remover, and there's no odor.

PICTURE FRAMES

To paint a picture frame without smudging the finish, first nail a piece of wood across the back of the frame. Use the wood as a handle when painting and remove it once the paint has dried.

SMALL PROJECTS

Use a paint mitt to quickly complete small projects. To make a mitt, put a disposable latex glove on your hand and then pull a fuzzy old sock over it. Dip this mitt into the paint and then coat your item with your hand in the mitt. The mitt makes it easy to paint nooks and crannies and, when you're done, you simply throw it away. *See illustration next page*

SPATTER REMOVAL

Keep a box of baby wipes nearby while you're painting. The wipes are great for removing fresh paint spatters from wood trim, glass, or uncarpeted floors.

To remove old paint spatters from windows, tile, or linoleum, put a little nail polish remover on a soft cloth and scrub the paint away.

SPRAY PAINT

To make spray paint easier to work with, set the can in warm water for a few minutes before using it. This helps the paint spray easier, resulting in a more even coat of paint.

Wrap your finger with a bit of plastic wrap to keep it clean when spray-painting.

When spraying a flat surface, begin spraying the side that is closest to you and work toward the opposite end. Use a steady, sweeping motion and cover the overspray with your next pass. That way your final finish will be smooth.

SPRAY PAINT, CLOG PREVENTION
To prevent clogging after use, hold the can upside down and spray out any remaining paint in the nozzle. This prevents the paint from drying in the nozzle and clogging it while in storage.

SPRAY PAINT, CUSTOM COLORS
If you can't find the right spray paint color, make your own. Buy a one-time aerosol-spray kit from a hardware or home improvement store. The kit includes a small glass bottle and a propellant canister. Add the paint of your choice and you're ready to go.

STAINING WOOD
To apply an oil- or water-based stain to untreated wood, use a cellulose sponge instead of a brush. It will be easier to control the amount you're applying.

Pour wood stain, oil, or polyurethane into an empty plastic dish-soap container for smaller jobs. This makes it easier to easier to squirt just a little when you're hand-rubbing finishes onto wood.

STORAGE

To prevent paint from drying out, cover the paint can with plastic wrap, replace the lid securely and store the can upside down. Store the paint where it won't freeze (once paint freezes, it can't be used again).

SWITCH PLATES

When you're finished painting a room, make a brief record of the paint job on the back of the switch plate. Include the date the room was painted, as well as the type, color, and brand of paint you used. If you ever need to match the paint, you'll have an easy reference.

TAPE

To make a dispenser for painting tape, cut the tube section out of an old sock. Slip the sock tube over your wrist and forearm and then slip the roll of tape over the sock. You'll be able to easily dispense the tape and free both hands to work.

See illustration next page

Remove painting tape from trim while the paint is still wet. This gives you a clean line and prevents the paint from peeling away with the tape.

TEMPORARY STORAGE

If you are in the middle of a painting project and need to stop temporarily, you can postpone cleaning the paintbrush by putting it into a zip-lock bag. Submerge the unsealed bag in water (without letting any into the bag) to remove as much air as possible. Then seal the bag and put it into the refrigerator.

You can do a similar trick with a roller brush by covering it in plastic wrap so that no air can get through to the paint. Then put the roller brush in the refrigerator. It should stay good for up to a week. If you need more time, put the brush in the freezer.

TIGHT SPOTS

Use a disposable cosmetic sponge to paint crevices and tight corners. To reach farther into hard-to-reach areas, tape a small piece of the sponge to the end of a screwdriver or pencil.

TOUCH-UP KITS

Make a small touch-up kit by putting some of the left-over paint into a small jar. Mark the jar with the type, color, and brand of paint, as well as the room in which it was used.

UNDERCOAT

When painting dark interior woodwork white, first apply a coat of aluminum paint. After this, you'll only need one coat of white paint or enamel to cover the woodwork.

WINDOW FRAMES

If you're painting a window frame, paint over the putty at least an eighth of an inch onto the glass. This will keep the putty anchored to the glass and prevent moisture from creeping in behind the putty and rotting your window sash.

Plumbing

CISTERN OVERFLOW

Stop more water from entering an overflowing cistern by removing the cistern top and tying the lever arm to a slab of wood laid across the top of the cistern.

DRAIN CARE

To prevent clogs and foul-smelling drains, pour hot saltwater down your drains once a week. The salty solution will flush out any built-up grease.

Do not pour fat such as bacon grease down a drain. It will set in the "U" bend of the pipe. Instead, pour it into an old can, let it harden, and throw it away.

Do not dump coffee grounds down the sink. Discard them instead. *See illustration previous page*

DRAIN, CLOGGED

If the cover to your bathtub drain is difficult to remove, use an afghan hook (available at craft or fabric stores) to remove hair and other clogs.

Try using a half-cup plunger to unclog the drains in your bathroom sinks. It often works better than harsh chemicals, and it won't harm the environment. (Don't use the same plunger that you use for toilets. Keep one plunger for toilets and another for sinks.) First, remove the sink stopper. Next, plug the bathtub or sink overflow with a rag. Press the plunger over the drain and run water over the top. Turn off the water and use a quick up-and-down motion to free the clog.

In kitchen sinks, grease buildup in the trap is the most likely cause of a clogged drain. Use a hair dryer or heat lamp to warm the trap. This should melt the grease. Next, flush the drain with very hot water.

FAUCET, LEAKING

If you don't have the specific size washer needed to repair a leaking faucet, cut a temporary washer from a plastic lid and use it to replace the old washer. The repair should last a few months.

FAUCET, SQUEAKY

If your faucet squeaks when you turn the handle, the metal threads of the stem are bending against the threads of the faucet. Remove the handle and stem, and coat both sets of threads with petroleum jelly.

PIPES, FREEZE PREVENTION

Keep your pipes from freezing during cold snaps by doing the following:

Keep a trickle of water running from the faucets.

Direct a space heater or heat lamp at exposed pipes.

Keep the doors open between heated and unheated rooms.

Insulate exposed pipes.

PIPES, FROZEN

A faucet that won't supply water is the first sign of frozen pipes. Act fast and you can thaw the pipes before they burst.

To thaw a frozen pipe, turn off the main supply valve. Open all faucets connected to the frozen pipe so it can drain as it thaws. Apply heat using a hair dryer or by wrapping a heating pad around the pipe. Work from the faucet toward the iced-up area.

See illustration previous page

If a waste line is frozen, pour boiling saltwater down the drain or apply heat to the line.

SHUT-OFF VALVE

To keep your shut-off valve from becoming locked into place, turn the handles off and on twice a year.

SHUT-OFF VALVE, STUCK

Do not force the handle of a shut-off valve that's stuck. Use an old toothbrush to apply a calcium, lime and rust remover (available at hardware or home improvement stores). Try the handle again. If it works, spray the valve with WD-40®. If the handle is still stuck, the valve is probably corroded shut and needs to be replaced. Call a professional.

TOILET, LEAKING

Your toilet is leaking if you observe one or more of the following signs:

The toilet makes sounds when it's not in use, such as intermittently running for no apparent reason.

You have to jiggle the handle to get the toilet to stop running.

You see water trickling down the sides of the bowl long after the toilet has been flushed.

To diagnose one common problem, put several drops of green food coloring into the tank. Wait 30 minutes, and then check the toilet bowl. If you see green, the ball at the bottom of the tank is not sealing properly.

TOILET, NOT FLUSHING

Most toilet clogs can be removed with a plunger. Avoid using chemical clog removers – they work best on grease clogs.

If the toilet is not clogged, check the tank. If the water level seems low, adjust it by raising the float. Then use a small mirror to check the water ports under the toilet rim. If the ports are clogged with mineral deposits, clean them out with a wire coat hanger dipped in white vinegar. Flush the toilet to remove the loose deposits. You may need to do this a few times.

TOILET, PARTIAL FLUSH

If you have to hold the handle down while flushing a toilet, the lift chain inside the tank may simply be too long. Shorten it by hooking the upper end through a different trip lever.

WATER TANK NOISE

If you hear rumbling sounds coming from the tank of your hot water heater, it could be overheating. Turn off the burner immediately and call a plumber.

TOOLS AND EQUIPMENT

BOLT, RUSTED

To loosen a rusted bolt, soak a rag in Coke® or Pepsi® and hold it on the bolt. It should loosen in a few minutes. Before you screw the bolt back on, coat it with petroleum jelly to prevent more rust.

BROOMS, CLEANING

Use hot, soapy water to clean a broom. Rinse thoroughly and wrap a rubber band around the bristles until they're completely dry. The rubber band will help the bristles keep their shape.

BROOMS, MAINTENANCE

Tighten the handle on a push broom by wrapping heavy-duty tape around the worn threads. Then simply screw the threads back into the broom head.

To make an outdoor broom last longer, dip the ends of the bristles into a shallow dish of thinned shellac. The bristles last longer on rough cement or patio stones.

BROOMS, STORAGE

Store a broom by hanging it up off the floor. This will help the bristles keep their shape.

DRILLS

To keep a bit on target, first make a starter dimple by

tapping a screw or other sharp-pointed object in the desired location.

To avoid drilling completely through a piece of wood, measure and mark the correct depth with a piece of tape on your drill bit.

If your goal is to make a large hole, first drill a small hole and then gradually enlarge it until it's the desired size.

Wrap duct tape around a drill bit that is a fitting too loosely into the drill.

DUSTPANS
Wet the edge of a newspaper and use it as a substitute for a dustpan.

To make a dustpan that also acts as a scraper, cut off a third of one side of an aluminum pie plate.

FLASHLIGHTS
Paint the handle of a flashlight with glow-in-the-dark paint to make it easy to find if the power goes out.

FUNNELS
Use old detergent or bleach bottles to make a funnel. Cut about 4 inches from the bottom of the bottle, remove the cap, and turn it upside down.

HAMMER, MAINTENANCE

Sand the face of your hammer periodically to roughen it up and keep it from sliding off nail heads and damaging your walls.

HINGES, SQUEAKY

To silence a squeaky hinge, spray it with shaving cream.

LADDER, WOOD

Drill a few holes into the top step of a wooden ladder to keep tools handy while you're working. Hang the tools in the holes. *See illustration*

To add more traction to the steps of the ladder, paint them and sprinkle sand in the wet paint.

LADDER, METAL
To keep tools handy while working on a metal ladder, attach a high-powered magnet to one of the legs. Set the tools on the magnet.

To make a non-skid surface on a metal ladder, first clean and dry the steps. Then apply drops of plastic rubber about 1 inch apart.

LUMBER, GRADING SCALE
When selecting lumber for a project, remember that lumber is measured on a grading scale. The higher the grade of the wood, the better looking and more resistant to decay and bugs it is.

MAGNET
Keep a small magnet nearby to make it easier to pick up small nails and screws.

MALLET
To make a mallet, cut a small X into an old tennis ball. Make the X just big enough to fit the ball over the head of a hammer.

MEASURING
Use a dollar bill to get a rough measurement if you don't have a tape measure handy. A dollar bill is approximately 6 inches long and 2.5 inches wide.

If you are measuring something and need to mark it, first place the pencil where you want to measure and then guide the straightedge to the pencil. This way, you don't have to compensate for the width of the pencil.

MEASURING TAPE
If you're working on a dusty project, keep your measuring tape clean by sliding an old toothbrush on the tape as it retracts.

NAILING OR SCREWING INTO HARDWOOD
To make it easier to get the screw or nail into the wood, first lubricate the tip with soap, oil, or grease.

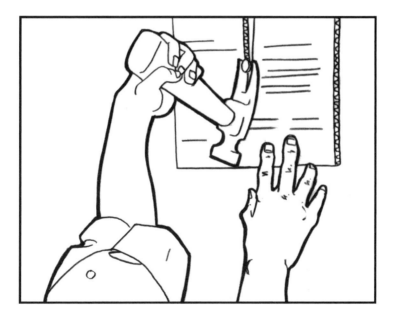

When removing a nail from a wall or other delicate surface, slip a piece of corrugated cardboard between the hammer and the wall. It will help protect the surface. *See illustration previous page*

NAIL STARTER
To avoid hitting your fingers when pounding in a nail, hold the nail with an old fork.

NUTS AND BOLTS
To prevent rust and make it easier to remove a bolt, rub paraffin wax on the threads before putting the nut on the bolt.

ORGANIZER, SMALL PARTS
Use an old cupcake pan to organize washers, nuts, and screws. For small parts, try using a plastic ice cube tray.

POWER OUTAGE
Put a dab of glow-in-the-dark spray paint on any tools (flashlights, etc.) that you might need during a power outage.

RUST PREVENTION
To prevent rust on your tools, put a few pieces of chalk, charcoal, or some mothballs in your toolbox to attract the moisture.

Spread a coat of petroleum jelly on tools that are not used often. It will keep them from getting rusty.

ROPE, UNSTIFFEN

Soak stiff rope in hot, soapy water until it becomes pliable. Hang to dry.

SANDING

To keep sandpaper handy, attach it to a clipboard and hang it on the wall near your workbench.

Sand with the grain of the wood to avoid leaving scratches on it.

Use a sanding sponge on rounded edges. If you don't have a sanding sponge, make one by wrapping sandpaper around a deck of cards. Press the vertical edge of the deck against the rounded edge. The cards will conform to the surface. *See illustration previous page*

Use an emery board to sand small or hard-to-reach areas.

SAWHORSE, TEMPORARY

To make a temporary sawhorse, use a ladder and a short board. Put the board on the second rung of the ladder and position it so that it forms an angle with the floor. Then set the piece of lumber you want to saw on the board with one side against the ladder.

SCREWS

To hold a screw in place until you get it started, tape the screw to the screwdriver using a piece of masking tape.

If you need to use a screwdriver in a tight spot, put a screwdriver bit into a one-fourth inch wrench.

Use an ice pick to start a screw hole by gently tapping it into the spot where you want to put the screw. In hard surfaces like plaster or hardwood, use a hammer to tap the ice pick.

Rub wax or soap over the threads of a screw before using it to make it penetrate more easily and be less likely to split the wood.

Dip screws in glue before tightening to keep them from loosening.

SCREWS, STRIPPED

Put a little putty into the grooves of a screwdriver to prevent it from slipping off the head of a screw that has been stripped.

STAPLE REMOVER

If you can't find the staple remover, try using fingernail clippers.

STEEL WOOL

To avoid getting poked by steel wool, clamp the wool with thick paper.

STUD FINDER

Use an electric razor to find studs in the walls. Listen

to the sound the razor makes as you rub it over the wall. The tone will change when you pass over a stud.
See illustration previous page

TOOL HANGER
Use a C clamp as a tool hanger when working on a ladder. Clamp it to a side rail.

WALLS AND CEILINGS

ACOUSTIC TILE

To clean, vacuum with a brush attachment. Remove small stains with wallpaper cleaner or a little soapy water on a cloth.

To fix loose or bulging acoustical tiles applied to wood furring strips, nail them to the strips with flat-head nails. If the tiles are applied on plaster, use cement-coated nails, countersink the nailheads, and cover them with spackle.

BASEMENT WALLS

Paint basement walls with fungus- and mildew-resistant paint.

Do not use vinyl wallpaper on basement walls because it can trap moisture. Use porous wallpaper that will allow moisture to pass though.

CEILINGS, CLEANING

To remove cobwebs from a vaulted ceiling, put a tennis ball in a sock and gently toss it at the cobwebs. It may take a few tries, but you'll be able to knock down the cobwebs. *See illustration next page*

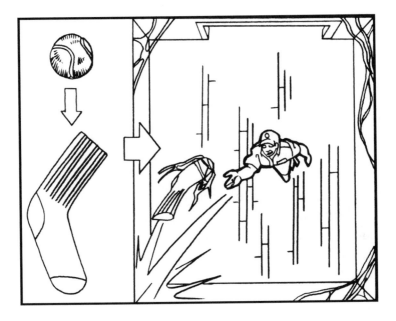

CEILINGS, DRILLING

To avoid getting showered in dust when drilling a hole into the ceiling, first drill a small hole through the center of a plastic cup. Put the cup flush with the ceiling while you drill, and it will contain the dust.

COVERAGE, PAINT OR WALLPAPER

To determine how much paint or wallpaper you'll need to cover a wall, determine the square footage of the wall. Then divide the area of the wall by the coverage of a single roll of wallpaper or a can of paint as noted on the label. Buy slightly more than you think you'll need so that you'll have enough to touch up scratches or blemishes later.

CRAYON MARKS, REMOVAL
Use a little WD-40® on a soft cloth to remove crayon marks from the walls. When the marks are gone, apply dish soap directly on the area with a soft cloth to clean the lubricant away. Then rinse the area with warm water.

DRYWALL, PATCHING
Apply three coats of spackle when patching drywall. Allow each coat to dry before applying the next. Each coat should cover a wider area and be smoother than the previous one, so that the patch will not show after it's painted. Make the third coat as smooth as possible so it will need little sanding.

MOISTURE DAMAGE, DETERMINING CAUSE
To find out if a moisture problem is caused by condensation or seepage, tape a piece of aluminum foil to the wall. Remove the foil after three days. If the room side of the foil is wet, the problem is condensation. If the wall side is wet, the culprit is seepage. Keep in mind that both problems can happen at the same time.

PICTURES, HANGING
Rub a little chalk on your finger to mark the nail hole when you're getting ready to hang a picture. The chalk is easy to wipe off, and you won't need to juggle a pencil while you're holding the picture.

If you hammer a nail in the wall and miss the stud, bend a metal clothes hanger and stick it in the hole in the wall. Spin the hanger to the left and right to find the stud before making any more holes in the wall.

If a picture frame is missing the hardware needed to hang it, glue or staple the tab of a soda can onto the back of the frame. *See illustration*

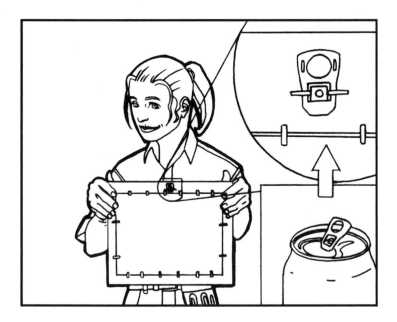

PLASTER, NAILING INTO
To reduce the risk of cracking or crumbling plaster, first warm the nail in hot water or dip it into melted paraffin.

PLASTER, PATCHING
Make a scraper from bottle caps nailed to a piece of wood and use it to roughen plaster before patching it.

SCUFF MARKS
Use a dry gum eraser to clean scuff marks from the wall. If that doesn't erase the mark, try wiping the marks away with a little toothpaste (not the gel kind) on a damp cloth.

WATER DRIPS
Stop a water drip in the ceiling from spreading along the ceiling board by tapping a nail in near the source of the drip. Put a bucket below. The water will drip down the nail and into the bucket.

WALLS, CLEANING
Use a natural sponge to clean painted walls or paneling. To make a good cleaning solution, mix one-half cup ammonia, one-fourth cup white vinegar, and one-fourth washing soda (available in the laundry section) in a gallon of warm water.

Do not use water to clean woven wallpaper; it will weaken the fibers, causing them to rip or stain. Instead, vacuum it using a brush attachment.

WALLS, MEASURING
Use a piece of sandpaper to keep a level from slipping
when you're marking a horizontal line on the wall.
Fold the sandpaper with the grit side out and put it
between the level and the wall.

WALLPAPER, FABRIC
Spray the fabric with water to get the wrinkles out.

WEIGHTS AND MEASUREMENTS

CONVERTING COOKING MEASUREMENTS
(U.S.)

A pinch or dash (dry) = Less than 1/8 teaspoon

A dash (liquid) = A few drops

3 teaspoons = 1 tablespoon

1/2 tablespoon = 1 1/2 teaspoons

1 tablespoon = 3 teaspoons

2 tablespoons = 1 fluid ounce

4 tablespoons = 1/4 cup

5 1/3 tablespoons = 1/3 cup

8 tablespoons = 1/2 cup

8 tablespoons = 4 fluid ounces

10 2/3 tablespoons = 2/3 cup

12 tablespoons = 3/4 cup

16 tablespoons = 1 cup

16 tablespoons = 8 fluid ounces

1/8 cup = 2 tablespoons

1/4 cup = 4 tablespoons

1/4 cup = 2 fluid ounces

1/3 cup = 5 tablespoons plus 1 teaspoon

1/2 cup = 8 tablespoons

1 cup = 16 tablespoons

1 cup = 8 fluid ounces

1 cup = 1/2 pint

2 cups = 1 pint

2 pints = 1 quart

4 quarts (liquid) = 1 gallon

8 quarts (dry) = 1 peck

4 pecks (dry) = 1 bushel

1 kilogram = Approximately 2 pounds
1 liter = Approximately 4 cups or 1 quart

CONVERTING LINEAR MEASUREMENTS

12 inches = 1 foot
3 feet = 1 yard
8 furlongs = 1 statute mile = 1,760 yards = 5,280 feet
3 land miles = 1 league
5,280 feet = 1 statute or land mile
6,076.11549 feet = 1 international nautical mile

CONVERTING AREA MEASUREMENTS

144 square inches = 1 square foot
9 square feet = 1 square yard = 1,296 square inches
30 1/4 square yards = 272 1/4 square feet
1 acre = 4,840 square yards = 43,560 square feet
640 acres = 1 square mile

CONVERTING CUBIC MEASUREMENTS

1,728 cubic inches = 1 cubic foot
27 cubic feet = 1 cubic yard